MW01153264

MONSTER Ships

by Chris Bowman

BELLWETHER MEDIA • MINNEAPOLIS, MN

Note to Librarians, Teachers, and Parents:

Blastoff! Readers are carefully developed by literacy experts and combine standards-based content with developmentally appropriate text.

Level 1 provides the most support through repetition of high-frequency words, light text, predictable sentence patterns, and strong visual support.

Level 2 offers early readers a bit more challenge through varied simple sentences, increased text load, and less repetition of high-frequency words.

Level 3 advances early-fluent readers toward fluency through increased text and concept load, less reliance on visuals, longer sentences, and more literary language.

Level 4 builds reading stamina by providing more text per page, increased use of punctuation, greater variation in sentence patterns, and increasingly challenging vocabulary.

Level 5 encourages children to move from "learning to read" to "reading to learn" by providing even more text, varied writing styles, and less familiar topics.

Whichever book is right for your reader, Blastoff! Readers are the perfect books to build confidence and encourage a love of reading that will last a lifetime!

This edition first published in 2014 by Bellwether Media, Inc.

No part of this publication may be reproduced in whole or in part without written permission of the publisher. For information regarding permission, write to Bellwether Media, Inc., Attention: Permissions Department, 5357 Penn Avenue South, Minneapolis, MN 55419.

Library of Congress Cataloging-in-Publication Data

Bowman, Chris, 1990-
  Monster Ships / by Chris Bowman.
     pages cm. – (Blastoff! Readers: Monster Machines)
  Includes bibliographical references and index.
  Summary: "Developed by literacy experts for students in kindergarten through grade three, this book introduces ships to young readers through leveled text and related photos"– Provided by publisher.
  Audience: Ages 5-8.
  Audience: Grades K to 3.
  ISBN 978-1-62617-054-4 (hbk. : alk. paper)
  1. Ships–Juvenile literature. I. Title.
  VM150.B66 2014
  623.82'04–dc23
                    2013035106

Printed in the United States of America, North Mankato, MN.

Table of Contents

Monster Ships!

Many ships move heavy **cargo**. These ships are huge!

cargo

The biggest ships can hold 18,000 large cargo boxes!

Supertankers carry **oil**. The longest ship ever built was a supertanker.

Cruise ships take people on vacations. They have big swimming pools on board.

Propellers and Engines

Giant **propellers** move big ships through water.

propellers

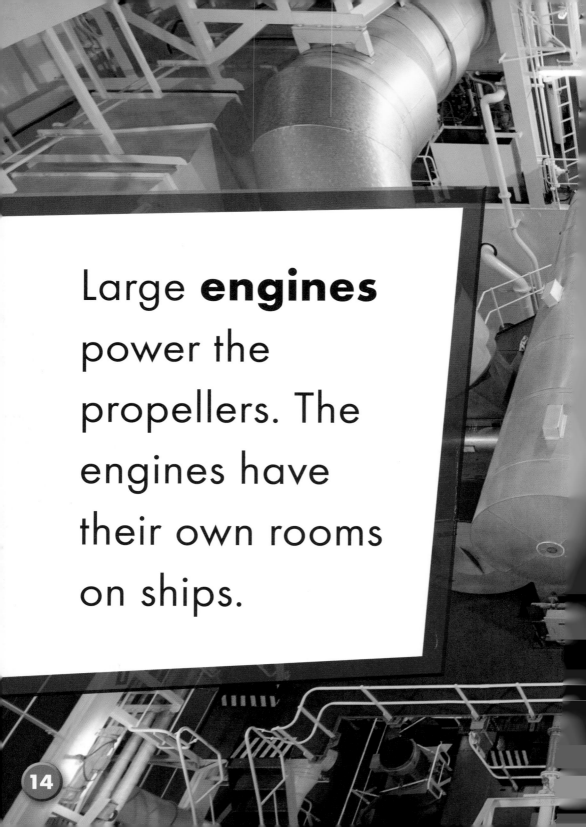

Large **engines** power the propellers. The engines have their own rooms on ships.

The world's fastest ship has **jet engines**.

jet engines

Aircraft carriers are the biggest **military** ships ever built.

One aircraft carrier can hold up to 90 airplanes!

Glossary

aircraft carriers—military ships that hold airplanes

cargo—goods that are carried by an airplane, ship, or truck

engines—machines that power vehicles

jet engines—machines that often power airplanes

military—relating to soldiers and war

oil—fuel that can be made into gasoline

propellers—blades that spin in the water to move a ship forward

supertankers—huge ships that carry large amounts of oil

To Learn More

AT THE LIBRARY

Doeden, Matt. *Aircraft Carriers*. Minneapolis, Minn.: Lerner Publications Co., 2006.

Kentley, Eric, and David Hawcock. *The Pop-up Book of Ships*. New York, N.Y.: Universe Publications, 2009.

Stewart, Melissa. *Titanic*. Washington, D.C.: National Geographic, 2012.

ON THE WEB

Learning more about ships is as easy as 1, 2, 3.

1. Go to www.factsurfer.com.

2. Enter "ships" into the search box.

3. Click the "Surf" button and you will see a list of related Web sites.

With factsurfer.com, finding more information is just a click away.

Index

The images in this book are reproduced through the courtesy of:
Michael Haul/ Getty Images, front cover; photoinnovation, pp. 4-5;
tcly, pp. 6-7; Gordon Bell, pp. 8-9; Isantilli, pp. 10-11; Ruth Peterkin,
p. 11 (small); Faraways, pp. 12-13; Sean Gallup/ Getty Images,
p. 12 (small); acincin, pp. 14-15; Robert Heazlewood/ Incat,
pp. 16-17, 17 (small); Hugh Gentry/ Reuters/ Newscom, pp. 18-19;
Department of Defense, pp. 20-21.